ENCOUNTERING JESUS

8 studies
for individuals or groups

Douglas Connelly

With Notes for Leaders

Scripture Union

We are an international Christian charity working with churches in more than 130 countries providing resources to bring the good news about Jesus Christ to children, young people and families – and to encourage them to develop spiritually through the Bible and prayer.

As well as our network of volunteers, staff and associates who run holidays, church-based events and school Christian groups, we produce a wide range of publications and support those who use our resources through training programmes.

Scripture Union, 207–209 Queensway, Bletchley, MK2 2EB, England
e-mail: info@scriptureunion.org.uk
website: www.scriptureunion.org.uk

©2002 by Douglas Connelly

First published in the United States by InterVarsity Press
First published in Great Britain by Scripture Union, 2002

Cover photograph: Dennis Flaherty

ISBN 1-85999-408-3

Printed in Great Britain by Ebenezer Baylis & Son Ltd., The Trinity Press, Worcester and London

Contents

Getting the Most Out of *Encountering Jesus*

Eight changed lives! Four men and four women. A scholar, a failure, a blind man and an adulteress. Their lives were changed forever because they came in contact with one incredible person—Jesus Christ.

Looking at these lives gives us hope because we find ourselves in some of the same situations. We may be caught in the grip of bad choices or living in the backwash of failure. We may be outstanding members of the community but sense an emptiness in life that possessions and position can't fill. We may find ourselves in a physical condition or in a marriage relationship that seems impossible to change.

The good news is that Jesus can change us no matter what our life situation. He can give us peace and hope and joy in the most desperate circumstances. But we need a life-changing encounter with him—whether it's for the first time or to renew an old friendship. He's waiting to meet us—around the corner, in the coffee shop, as we cruise along the highway. But be prepared. You may come away from that encounter like these eight people did—with your life transformed!

Suggestions for Individual Study

1. As you begin each study, pray that God will speak to you through his Word.

2. Read the introduction to the study and respond to the "personal reflection" question or exercise. This is designed to help you focus on God and on the theme of the study.

3. Each study deals with a particular passage—so that you can delve into the author's meaning in that context. Read and reread the passage to be studied. If you are studying a book, it will be helpful to read through the entire book prior to the first study. The questions are written using the language of the New International Version, so you may wish to use that version of the Bible. The New Revised Standard Version is also recommended.

4. This is an inductive Bible study, designed to help you discover for yourself what Scripture is saying. The study includes three types of questions. *Observation* questions ask about the basic facts: who, what, when, where and how. *Interpretation* questions delve into the meaning of the passage. *Application* questions help you discover the implications of the text for growing in Christ. These three keys unlock the treasures of Scripture.

Write your answers to the questions in the spaces provided or in a personal journal. Writing can bring clarity and deeper understanding of yourself and of God's Word.

5. It might be good to have a Bible dictionary handy. Use it to look up any unfamiliar words, names or places.

6. Use the prayer suggestion to guide you in thanking God for what you have learned and to pray about the applications that have come to mind.

7. You may want to go on to the suggestion under "Now or Later," or you may want to use that idea for your next study.

Suggestions for Members of a Group Study

1. Come to the study prepared. Follow the suggestions for individual study mentioned above. You will find that careful preparation will greatly enrich your time spent in group discussion.

2. Be willing to participate in the discussion. The leader of your group will not be lecturing. Instead, he or she will be encouraging the members of the group to discuss what they have learned. The leader will be asking the questions that are found in this guide.

3. Stick to the topic being discussed. Your answers should be based on the verses which are the focus of the discussion and not on outside authorities such as commentaries or speakers. These studies focus on a particular passage of Scripture. Only rarely should you refer to other portions of the Bible. This allows for everyone to participate in in-depth study on equal ground.

4. Be sensitive to the other members of the group. Listen attentively when they describe what they have learned. You may be surprised by their insights! Each question assumes a variety of answers. Many questions do not have "right" answers, particularly questions that aim at meaning or application. Instead the questions push us to explore the passage more thoroughly.

When possible, link what you say to the comments of others. Also, be affirming whenever you can. This will encourage some of the more hesitant members of the group to participate.

5. Be careful not to dominate the discussion. We are sometimes so eager to express our thoughts that we leave too little opportunity for others to respond. By all means participate! But allow others to also.

6. Expect God to teach you through the passage being discussed and through the other members of the group. Pray that you will have an enjoyable and profitable time together, but also that as a result of the study you will find ways that you can take action individually and/or as a group.

7. Remember that anything said in the group is considered confidential and should not be discussed outside the group unless specific permission is given to do so.

8. If you are the group leader, you will find additional suggestions at the back of the guide.

1

Water for
the Thirsty

Most of us think we know what will make us happy. Usually the list includes a new car or house. And we'd like to get our debts paid off. It might include a different job. Or perhaps we are looking for a new relationship to bring fulfillment.

GROUP DISCUSSION. Take turns describing a favorite commercial. What does that commercial offer or promise?

PERSONAL REFLECTION. If Jesus came unannounced to your home or workplace or favorite coffee shop and sat down beside you, what would he say to you about the ways you are looking for fulfilment?

We sometimes get the impression that Jesus was always surrounded by crowds of people. But Jesus was also concerned for the individual man or woman who was searching for peace. In John 4 Jesus connects with a woman whose search for fulfilment was about to end. *Read John 4:1-30.*

1. Consider what this situation must have felt like to the woman. How do you respond when someone speaks to you unexpectedly?

What if the person starts talking about religious issues?

2. Scan through the passage again and list all the individuals or groups of people who are mentioned. After each listing, note a few words that describe them, based on what you find in the passage itself.

3. Jesus' request for water surprises the Samaritan woman (vv. 7-9) because of their gender and ethnic differences. What present-day situations might arouse the same racial, religious or gender prejudices?

4. What does the woman think Jesus means when he talks about "living water" (vv. 10-15)?

What does he really mean?

5. Why do you think Jesus changes the subject to focus on the woman's personal life (vv. 16-18)?

_____

6. How does the conversation shift again in verses 19 and 20, and why do you think it happens?

_____

7. How do you think the woman feels when she hears that God is searching for people like her to worship him (vv. 21-24)?

_____

8. What principles can you draw from Jesus' conversation with the woman to help you in reaching out to others?

_____

9. Do you think the woman believed in Jesus? Support your answer with evidence from the passage.

_____

10. How does this study challenge or expand your picture of what it means to follow Jesus?

Ask God to give you a sensitive heart to people who need to be shown Jesus' love—and the courage to overcome the barriers that might prevent you from connecting with them.

Now or Later

11. Read "the rest of the story" in John 4:39-42. What impact did this woman's faith have on her community?

12. Do you think a commitment to Jesus is a personal issue or something to talk about with other people? Why?

13. What risks did the woman take as she shared her belief in Jesus as the Messiah?

2

Searching for Truth

John 3:1-21

The young man sitting across the table from me was searching. He had been raised in a religious family and had gone to church all his life. He had read the Bible, said his prayers regularly and fulfilled all the religious requirements asked of him. Yet he felt empty.

I was able to speak from my own experience when I described how real spiritual life is found in a relationship, not in religious activity. He already knew a lot about Jesus, so I just reminded him of what Jesus had done for him. As he opened his heart in faith to believe in Jesus and to commit to following Jesus, he experienced a spiritual birth. That decision set him on a new path—his new life was not perfect, but even in the ups and downs of life he found a deep sense of satisfaction in his relationship with Christ.

GROUP DISCUSSION. What religious activities have you tried throughout your life?

What has brought you satisfaction?

PERSONAL REFLECTION. Do you find more of your personal spiritual satisfaction in a relationship with Jesus or in religious activity? Why?

A very religious man came to see Jesus one night. He had been to the best schools and held a position of leadership in the Jewish community. The problem was the emptiness in his life. He came seeking information, but Jesus offered him transformation. *Read John 3:1-21.*

1. On a scale from totally confused about Jesus to totally committed to Jesus, where would you place Nicodemus at the beginning of this conversation?

On the same scale, where do you think Nicodemus is when he goes away?

2. Why do you think Nicodemus goes to see Jesus at night?

Why does he go at all?

In what ways can you relate to Nicodemus's approach to Jesus?

3. How is the concept of birth that Jesus is trying to explain different from what Nicodemus is thinking of (vv. 3-4)?

4. Based on what Jesus says in verses 5-8, how would you define the phrase "born again" (v. 7) to someone who had never heard it or who had a misconception about it?

5. In verse 14 Jesus refers back to a story in the Old Testament when Moses made a bronze snake and lifted it up among the people of Israel. God had sent poisonous snakes into Israel as a judgment on the people for their sin. Whoever looked at the bronze serpent in faith was delivered from death and judgment. (The story is in Numbers 21:4-9.) How does that story illustrate our spiritual need and what Jesus came to do?

6. What is your impression of God as you read verses 16-18?

7. How do the conditions for receiving eternal life in verses 16-18 contrast with the idea of gaining God's approval by doing good deeds?

What is appealing about the perspective that says we can earn God's approval?

8. According to verses 19-21, why doesn't everyone believe in Jesus and receive eternal life?

How do you feel as you read these verses?

9. Nicodemus's encounter with Jesus emphasizes our personal response and commitment to Jesus. How would you describe your own relationship with Jesus?

Thank Jesus for his willingness to open the door to eternal life to you.

Now or Later
If the beginning of a relationship with Jesus can be compared to a birth, think about the other lifestages of the relationship. What should characterise spiritual childhood? (1 Peter 2:2-3 may give you some insight.)
Spiritual adolescence? (Check out 1 Peter 1:14-16.)
Spiritual maturity? (Read Ephesians 4:13.)
Where would you put yourself on the growing-up scale?

3

Caught in
the Act

John 8:1-11

When I turned the corner, both of us were startled. As a grocery store assistant working my way through college, I had dealt with my share of shoplifters, but this one was a pro. The large pockets inside her coat held packages of steaks, cartons of cigarettes and several bottles of pain relievers. As I stepped into the grocery store aisle, she was trying to put the last package of meat into the pocket, and it just wouldn't fit. When she looked up, she knew she had been caught in the act.

GROUP DISCUSSION. What wrongs do we tend to look at as the "big" ones— the sins that are worse than all others?

Which sins do you think God looks at as the big sins?

PERSONAL REFLECTION. What wrongs do you think you could never commit?

How do you usually respond to people who have committed those sins?

Nothing is more humiliating than being caught in the act of doing wrong. Whether it's a child with a hand in the cookie jar or an adult driving over the speed limit, we all know the sinking feeling of being caught. In John 8, a woman is caught in the most awkward of situations—in the very act of adultery. She is pulled from the bed and pushed into the sunlight in front of Jesus. His response may surprise you. *Read John 8:1-11.*

1. If you were a reporter covering this event, which scenes would you select to show on the nightly news?

Which person would you most want to interview after the incident ended, and what question would you ask first?

2. The woman is forced to stand before a whole crowd while her sin is publicly exposed. How do you feel when someone confronts you in front of others?

3. Verse 6 says this confrontation was planned as a way to trap Jesus. What evidence do you find in the story that this was a setup?

4. What accusation would the Pharisees bring against Jesus if he told them to let the woman go?

What would the people think of Jesus if he told the Pharisees to stone her?

---

5. Why do you think Jesus writes in the dirt when he is pressed for an answer (v. 6)?

---

6. The Pharisees and teachers of the law are rigid rule-keepers. The woman is guilty, and the law of Moses clearly condemns her. Why don't they stone her (vv. 7-9)?

---

7. Why do we find it easier to condemn wrongdoing in others than in ourselves?

---

8. Is Jesus condoning the woman's sin by not condemning her? Explain.

9. How does Jesus' treatment of the woman help you face sin in your own life?

_____

10. What can you learn from Jesus' example about helping a friend who has done something wrong—even one of the "big" sins?

Thank God for his forgiveness and his grace to you.

Now or Later

Honestly examining our lives before God is never easy. Carve out some time this week to think through your actions, attitudes, relationships and thought patterns. You might want to read Psalm 51 prayerfully as you begin. Ask God to examine your heart and reveal anything that is not pleasing to him. Confess areas where you need to be more obedient to God. Use a journal to write down some first steps to change in those areas. Share your goals with a trusted Christian friend who can hold you accountable for those goals.

4

Finding
Forgiveness

Luke 7:36-50

When he was ten years old, Christopher Carrier was kidnapped by a man who said he knew Chris's father. Actually the man did know Chris's father because he had just been fired by him. To get revenge, the man took his boss's young son, stabbed and shot him, and then left him for dead in the Florida Everglades. Amazingly, Chris survived that ordeal. But he was never able to positively identify his attacker. Finally, twenty-two years after the crime, Chris's attacker, David McCallister, confessed to the police.

Even more amazing was Chris's desire to visit McCallister in the nursing home where he was dying. McCallister was now almost eighty years old, weak and blind. Chris introduced himself, and McCallister confessed again but this time directly to the person he had tried to kill so long before. In a tearful scene of reconciliation, Chris Carrier forgave the man who had terrorized his life.*

---

*National Public Radio interview broadcast October 13, 1996.

GROUP DISCUSSION. In what other ways could Chris Carrier have responded to his attacker, and what results would have come from each possible response?

PERSONAL REFLECTION. Do you think you would have responded the same way Chris Carrier did? Why or why not?

We do not live in a culture of forgiveness. We are far more concerned with revenge. Jesus sat down for a meal one evening with a bunch of critical, judgmental people who were intent only on embarrassing him. Jesus, however, turned the tables on them when a woman showed up—a woman who had found forgiveness. *Read Luke 7:36-50.*

1. Imagine yourself as a guest at Simon's party. What seems to be Simon's main concern as events unfold in this passage?

What about Jesus' main concern?

What is the woman's main concern?

2. What conclusion does Simon come to about Jesus (v. 39)?

3. In Jesus' story, one debtor owed the equivalent of two years' salary, and the other debtor owed the equivalent of two months' salary. Which debtor represents the woman and which represents Simon? Explain.

What is Jesus trying to get Simon to realize by telling him the story?

4. Simon had not just *forgotten* to welcome Jesus as a guest by not giving him water to wash his feet (vv. 44-46). Simon had deliberately *refused* to treat Jesus as a friend. What do his actions reveal about the kind of person Simon really is?

5. What do the woman's actions reveal about what had happened in her life because of an encounter with Jesus (vv. 44-47)?

6. Which person in the story do you most closely identify with, and why?

7. Do you think Simon is changed by this episode? Explain why or why not.

8. How do you think the woman feels when she hears Jesus' words of forgiveness and peace (vv. 48, 50)?

9. How do you think the woman's lifestyle changes, and what motivates her to change?

10. Based on the example of this woman, how can you demonstrate your gratitude to Jesus for forgiving you?

Thank God for forgiving you of your debt of sin. Imagine Jesus saying to you, "Your sins are forgiven. Go in peace."

Now or Later

Jesus often uses images to picture the spiritual changes he brings to those who believe in him. Think about these images and the spiritual needs that Jesus can fill in your life.

■ "I am the bread of life. He who comes to me will never go hungry" (John 6:35).

■ "I am the good shepherd; I know my sheep and my sheep know me" (John 10:14).

■ "I am the way and the truth and the life. No one comes to the Father except through me" (John 14:6).

■ "I am the vine; you are the branches. If a man remains in me and I in him, he will bear much fruit" (John 15:5).

5

Facing Failure

At one time in my life God seemed very far away. I was living in the backwash of personal failure and sin. I knew God had forgiven me, but it seemed like he didn't want to be my friend anymore. I felt like God was distant and unconcerned. I also wondered if God would ever allow me to be involved in ministry again. I'd blown it once. Maybe God would just set me aside and the work of building his kingdom would go on without me.

GROUP DISCUSSION. How do you respond to failure in other people?

How do you respond to failure in your own life?

PERSONAL REFLECTION. Think back to a time of failure in your life. What did it take for you to feel forgiven and restored?

Peter's failures are recorded in the Bible for everyone to read. As one of Jesus' closest followers, Peter vowed repeatedly that he would never abandon his friend. But when Jesus was arrested, Peter (like all of Jesus' followers) fled in terror. Prompted by guilt over his broken promise and motivated by concern for Jesus, Peter came to the courtyard outside the place where Jesus was being accused. When Peter was challenged about his association with Jesus, he denied even knowing the Lord—not once but three times.

In this passage at the end of John's Gospel, Peter faces Jesus again. Jesus has risen from the dead and is standing on the shore of the Sea of Galilee. Peter, in a fishing boat, wonders if Jesus will ever allow him to be part of building God's kingdom. Peter not only has to face Jesus; he also has to face his own failure and deepest fears. *Read John 21:1-19.*

---

1. What is Peter's emotional condition after fishing all night and catching nothing (v. 3)?

after hearing that the man on shore is Jesus (v. 7)?

after Jesus asks him three times about his love (vv. 15-17)?

after Jesus predicts Peter's helplessness at the time of his death (vv. 18-19)?

2. Do you think Peter just enjoys fishing, or is this a step back to his old career and way of life before he became a follower of Jesus? Explain why you came to that conclusion.

3. Earlier in his ministry, Jesus had guided his followers to a large catch of fish (Luke 5:1-11). Why would Jesus do the same thing in this situation (vv. 6-7)?

4. What would Jesus communicate to his disciples by preparing their breakfast and inviting them to eat?

5. Two different words for love are used in the exchange between Jesus and Peter in verses 15-17. When Jesus asks Peter, "Do you *truly love* me?" he uses a word referring to wholehearted, sacrificial commitment. Peter responds with a word that signifies deep affection but a weaker commitment than the love Jesus asks from him. What does this reveal about Peter?

6. If a close friend had abandoned you, how would you respond to this sort of less-than-total commitment later?

What does Peter discover about Jesus through Jesus' response to him (v. 15)?

_____

7. The third time Jesus asks his question he uses Peter's word for love—"Simon, son of John, do you *love* me?" Why does Jesus change the word?

Describe how the change affects Peter and why (v. 17).

_____

8. How would you honestly answer Jesus' three questions?

What would Jesus say to you in response?

9. In what ways will Jesus' words to Peter—"feed my sheep" (vv. 15, 17) and "follow me" (v. 19)—change the way you recover from failure in the future?

Seek Jesus' forgiveness for any failure. Thank him that he responds to you with grace and love.

Now or Later

Peter learned through his failure that he needed to be more open to the warnings and advice of other people. The same principle will help us head off serious failure in our own lives. Think of one or two people you can make yourself accountable to. These people should be mature Christians who will give you wise counsel and who will love you enough to ask hard questions. They should also be open and vulnerable enough to be accountable to you. Finding the right people and forming an accountability group is not an easy process, but it will pay solid dividends in your own spiritual growth.

6

Set Free

No one has to convince us that we live in an evil world. Just read the newspaper or watch the news! What might not be so obvious is that evil is sometimes promoted by powerful beings the Bible calls *demons*. These are not the little, horned, pitch-fork-carrying imps from the cartoons. Demons are intelligent, spiritual beings who operate under Satan's direction. Their goal is to oppress and deceive anyone they can. They plan their attacks very carefully. At times they grip a person's mind and body completely. Liberation comes only through an encounter with Jesus.

GROUP DISCUSSION. Do you believe demons are real?

PERSONAL REFLECTION. Think of the most evil person you know or know about. What would it be like to be forced to serve that person as a slave?

One day as Jesus stepped off a boat on the shore of the Sea of Galilee, he was met by the screams of an incredibly frightening man—a man dominated by evil spirits. *Read Mark 5:1-20.*

1. If you had witnessed this encounter between Jesus and the man, how do you think the people you work with would respond when you told them about it?

What parts of the account would they find most difficult to believe?

2. How would you feel if you lived near the man described in verses 1-5?

3. What would you pray for if the man were your brother or son?

4. When Jesus addresses the man in verses 6-9, who responds—the man or the demons? Explain.

5. What can you conclude from this passage about the physical, emotional and spiritual oppression that a person under demonic influence experiences?

What can you conclude about Jesus' power compared to the demons' powers?

6. What steps can we take to help someone who is oppressed by demonic forces?

7. Three requests are made of Jesus in the passage. How does he respond to the request of the demons (vv. 10-13)?

the request of the people in the area (vv. 14-17)?

the request of the restored man (vv. 18-19)?

8. What results can we expect to see when a person is set free from Satan's power (vv. 15, 19-20)?

———————————————————————————————

9. There may be an area of your life in which you sense evil influences are trying to gain control. What can you count on Jesus to do for you when you face evil?

Give praise to God that he protects you from the evil power of Satan (John 17:15) and that the Holy Spirit in you is greater than the enemy (1 John 4:4).

Now or Later
What testimony can you give about the liberating power of Jesus in your life?

Who would Jesus send you to tell?

7

Seeing
the Light

I earned extra money in college by working in a tutoring program. I got a call one day from another student who wanted my help, and I agreed to meet him that evening at his apartment. When I arrived and he opened the door, to my surprise the apartment was totally dark. I (reluctantly) went inside and he closed the door behind me. I heard him move a chair and shuffle some papers, but it was pitch black. Finally I said, "Do you always work in the dark?"

He said, "I'm sorry. I forgot to turn on a light. I'm blind—and to answer your question, yes, I *always* work in the dark."

GROUP DISCUSSION. What physical sense (seeing, hearing) or ability (walking, speaking) would it be most difficult for you to lose and why?

PERSONAL REFLECTION. What feelings or thoughts come over you when you see a person who is blind or confined to a wheelchair? Do you want to engage the person in a conversation or avoid the person?

As Jesus and his disciples entered the city of Jerusalem one day, they came upon a familiar sight. A blind man sat in the street begging for money. The disciples saw his blindness as a topic for debate. Jesus saw a person in need. Within a few minutes, the man's life was changed forever. *Read John 9:1-38.*

---

1. As you think about each person or group who plays a part in this unfolding drama—Jesus' disciples, the blind man, the crowd, the religious Pharisees, the man's parents—which of them are blind to God's work and which of them can see? Explain why you made your conclusions.

---

2. Based on the question they ask Jesus (v. 2), how do the disciples view this man and his condition?

How does Jesus see the man and his need?

---

3. What condition in your body or life could God use to display his glory and power?

4. What is revealed about the man when he simply obeys Jesus' instructions even though he has no idea who Jesus is?

5. On what grounds do the Pharisees object to this miracle (vv. 16, 22, 24, 29)?

6. What do their objections tell you about their spiritual condition?

7. How do you respond to people who try to be "religious" but who are quick to judge or condemn other people?

8. What do you learn from the man's response to the Pharisees about how to respond to people who ridicule your faith?

9. Why does Jesus seek out the healed man the second time (vv.

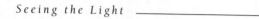
35-38)?

10. In what ways do you want Jesus to open your eyes and give you new spiritual sight?

Express your praise to Jesus as the Giver of true spiritual sight for giving you the ability to see him as your Saviour and God.

Now or Later

Jesus is "the light of the world" (John 9:5)—but Jesus also said that his followers were lights: "You are the light of the world" (Matthew 5:14). In what specific ways can you "let your light shine before men, that they may see your good deeds and praise your Father in heaven" (Matthew 5:16)?

8

When All
Else Fails

Luke 8:40-48

I was already running late as I hurried down the hospital corridor. The woman sitting in a wheelchair watched me intently as I approached. I gave her a weak smile and kept walking.

"Hey!" she shouted after me. "Are you a preacher?"

My first thought was *Is it that obvious*? My second thought was *I'll keep moving and pretend I didn't hear her*. The next thought was a gentle nudge from the Spirit of God. I stopped, turned around, walked back to her and said, "Yes, I am. Why do you ask?"

Her response broke my heart. "Why doesn't God heal me? I've prayed and prayed. I've promised God everything, but I don't get better. What more can I do?" Tears streamed down her cheeks, and sobs choked her words.

GROUP DISCUSSION. What would you have said to the woman in the hospital?

PERSONAL REFLECTION. Think about a time in your life (or in a friend's life) when you felt desperate. Where did you turn for help, and where did help ultimately come from?

In the middle of incredible demands and in the press of a large crowd, Jesus made room for one woman who found herself in a desperate situation. *Read Luke 8:40-48.*

---

1. What tone of voice do the following people use when they speak?

Jairus pleading for Jesus to come to his home (vv. 41-42)

Jesus asking who had touched him (v. 45)

Peter responding to Jesus' question (v. 45)

The woman telling her story (v. 47)

Jesus proclaiming the woman healed (v. 48)

---

2. What do we know about the woman in the crowd (v. 43)?

---

3. The law of the Old Testament said that a man or woman with a discharge of blood was ceremonially unclean (see Leviticus 15:19-33). This restricted their contact with other people and prohibited them from worship at the temple. What effect would those requirements of the law have had on this woman over a twelve-year span?

4. How does she demonstrate faith in Jesus and his power to heal her?

5. How does Jesus know that someone has been healed (vv. 45-46)?

6. What one thing in your life do you need Jesus to touch and restore?

7. The woman's affliction is so personal she doesn't want to approach Jesus directly. Why then does Jesus make the woman reveal herself publicly?

8. In what ways—other than physically—is the woman given peace?

9. How does this encounter make you feel about asking Jesus to bring healing to your life?

———————————————————————————

10. How will this passage help you show compassion for people with continuing physical needs or desperate personal problems?

———————————————————————————

11. What can you say to a person who has tried everything to change an impossible situation?

Ask God to touch your life (or a friend's life) to meet a specific need. Imagine Jesus saying to you, "Go in peace."

Now or Later
As you think back through these eight encounters Jesus had with individuals, in what specific ways has your perception of Jesus changed?

How has your awareness of his personal concern for you changed, and how will that new awareness affect how you approach Jesus?

Leader's Notes

Leading a Bible discussion can be an enjoyable and rewarding experience. But it can also be *scary*—especially if you've never done it before. If this is your feeling, you're in good company. When God asked Moses to lead the Israelites out of Egypt, he replied, "O Lord, please send someone else to do it"! (Ex 4:13). It was the same with Solomon, Jeremiah and Timothy, but God helped these people in spite of their weaknesses, and he will help you as well.

You don't need to be an expert on the Bible or a trained teacher to lead a Bible discussion. The idea behind these inductive studies is that the leader guides group members to discover for themselves what the Bible has to say. This method of learning will allow group members to remember much more of what is said than a lecture would.

These studies are designed to be led easily. As a matter of fact, the flow of questions through the passage from observation to interpretation to application is so natural that you may feel that the studies lead themselves. This study guide is also flexible. You can use it with a variety of groups—student, professional, neighborhood or church groups. Each study takes forty-five to sixty minutes in a group setting.

There are some important facts to know about group dynamics and encouraging discussion. The suggestions listed below should enable you to effectively and enjoyably fulfil your role as leader.

Preparing for the Study
1. Ask God to help you understand and apply the passage in your

own life. Unless this happens, you will not be prepared to lead others. Pray too for the various members of the group. Ask God to open your hearts to the message of his Word and motivate you to action.

2. Read the introduction to the entire guide to get an overview of the entire book and the issues which will be explored.

3. As you begin each study, read and reread the assigned Bible passage to familiarise yourself with it.

4. This study guide is based on the New International Version of the Bible. It will help you and the group if you use this translation as the basis for your study and discussion.

5. Carefully work through each question in the study. Spend time in meditation and reflection as you consider how to respond.

6. Write your thoughts and responses in the space provided in the study guide. This will help you to express your understanding of the passage clearly.

7. It might help to have a Bible dictionary handy. Use it to look up any unfamiliar words, names or places. (For additional help on how to study a passage, see chapter five of *Leading Bible Discussions*, InterVarsity Press.)

8. Consider how you can apply the Scripture to your life. Remember that the group will follow your lead in responding to the studies. They will not go any deeper than you do.

9. Once you have finished your own study of the passage, familiarize yourself with the leader's notes for the study you are leading. These are designed to help you in several ways. First, they tell you the purpose the study guide author had in mind when writing the study. Take time to think through how the study questions work together to accomplish that purpose. Second, the notes provide you with additional background information or suggestions on group dynamics for various questions. This information can be useful when people have difficulty understanding or answering a question. Third, the leader's notes can alert you to potential problems you may encounter during the study.

10. If you wish to remind yourself of anything mentioned in the leader's notes, make a note to yourself below that question in the study.

Leading the Study

1. Begin the study on time. Open with prayer, asking God to help the group to understand and apply the passage.

2. Be sure that everyone in your group has a study guide. Encourage the group to prepare beforehand for each discussion by reading the introduction to the guide and by working through the questions in the study.

3. At the beginning of your first time together, explain that these studies are meant to be discussions, not lectures. Encourage the members of the group to participate. However, do not put pressure on those who may be hesitant to speak during the first few sessions. You may want to suggest the following guidelines to your group.

■ Stick to the topic being discussed.

■ Your responses should be based on the verses which are the focus of the discussion and not on outside authorities such as commentaries or speakers.

■ These studies focus on a particular passage of Scripture. Only rarely should you refer to other portions of the Bible. This allows for everyone to participate in in-depth study on equal ground.

■ Anything said in the group is considered confidential and will not be discussed outside the group unless specific permission is given to do so.

■ We will listen attentively to each other and provide time for each person present to talk.

■ We will pray for each other.

4. Have a group member read the introduction at the beginning of the discussion.

5. Every session begins with a group discussion question. The question or activity is meant to be used before the passage is read. The question introduces the theme of the study and encourages group members to begin to open up. Encourage as many members as possible to participate, and be ready to get the discussion going with your own response.

This section is designed to reveal where our thoughts or feelings need to be transformed by Scripture. That is why it is especially important not to read the passage before the discussion question is asked. The passage will tend to color the honest reactions people would otherwise give because they are, of course, supposed to think the way the Bible does.

You may want to supplement the group discussion question with an icebreaker to help people to get comfortable. For more ideas, see Appendix A of *The Small-Group Leader* by John Mallison (Scripture Union).

You also might want to use the personal reflection question with your group. Either allow a time of silence for people to respond individually or discuss it together.

6. Have a group member (or members if the passage is long) read aloud the passage to be studied. Then give people several minutes to read the passage again silently so that they can take it all in.

7. Question 1 will generally be an overview question designed to briefly survey the passage. Encourage the group to look at the whole passage, but try to avoid getting sidetracked by questions or issues that will be addressed later in the study.

8. As you ask the questions, keep in mind that they are designed to be used just as they are written. You may simply read them aloud. Or you may prefer to express them in your own words.

There may be times when it is appropriate to deviate from the study guide. For example, a question may have already been answered. If so, move on to the next question. Or someone may raise an important question not covered in the guide. Take time to discuss it, but try to keep the group from going off on tangents.

9. Avoid answering your own questions. If necessary, repeat or rephrase them until they are clearly understood. Or point out something you read in the leader's notes to clarify the context or meaning. An eager group quickly becomes passive and silent if they think the leader will do most of the talking.

10. Don't be afraid of silence. People may need time to think about the question before formulating their answers.

11. Don't be content with just one answer. Ask, "What do the rest of you think?" or "Anything else?" until several people have given answers to the question.

12. Acknowledge all contributions. Try to be affirming whenever possible. Never reject an answer. If it is clearly off-base, ask, "Which

verse led you to that conclusion?" or again, "What do the rest of you think?"

13. Don't expect every answer to be addressed to you, even though this will probably happen at first. As group members become more at ease, they will begin to truly interact with each other. This is one sign of healthy discussion.

14. Don't be afraid of controversy. It can be very stimulating. If you don't resolve an issue completely, don't be frustrated. Move on and keep it in mind for later. A subsequent study may solve the problem.

15. Periodically summarize what the group has said about the passage. This helps to draw together the various ideas mentioned and gives continuity to the study. But don't preach.

16. At the end of the Bible discussion you may want to allow group members a time of quiet to work on an idea under "Now or Later." Then discuss what you experienced. Or you may want to encourage group members to work on these ideas between meetings. Give an opportunity during the session for people to talk about what they are learning.

17. Conclude your time together with conversational prayer, adapting the prayer suggestion at the end of the study to your group. Ask for God's help in following through on the commitments you've made.

18. End on time.

Many more suggestions and helps are found in *Leading Bible Discussions* (InterVarsity Press, USA).

Components of Small Groups

A healthy small group should do more than study the Bible. There are four components to consider as you structure your time together.

Nurture. Small groups help us to grow in our knowledge and love of God. Bible study is the key to making this happen and is the foundation of your small group.

Community. Small groups are a great place to develop deep friendships with other Christians. Allow time for informal interaction before and after each study. Plan activities and games that will help you get to know each other. Spend time having fun together—going on a picnic or cooking dinner together.

Worship and prayer. Your study will be enhanced by spending time praising God together in prayer or song. Pray for each other's needs—and keep track of how God is answering prayer in your group. Ask God to help you to apply what you are learning in your study.

Outreach. Reaching out to others can be a practical way of applying what you are learning, and it will keep your group from becoming self-focused. Host a series of evangelistic discussions for your friends or neighbors. Clean up the yard of an elderly friend. Serve at a soup kitchen together, or spend a day working on a Habitat house.

Many more suggestions and helps in each of these areas are found in *Small Group Idea Book.* Information on building a small group can be found in *Small Group Leaders' Handbook* and *The Big Book on Small Groups* (both from InterVarsity Press) and *The Small-Group Leader* and *Small Group Starter Kit* (both from Scripture Union). Reading through one of these books would be worth your time.

Leading a Group with Seekers
This guide is designed for use with those who want to learn more about Jesus, as well as with Christians. We have tried to write questions that are free of assumptions about the perspective of the group members. Further, we've focused on fact-based questions that deal with the text for those who don't have biblical background. And we've created application questions that would be appropriate to people in a variety of places in their understanding of Christ.

An engaging way to start each session is to use a video clip for your opening. Ideas to accompany each of these sessions are posted on the Web page for this book at <www.ivpress.com>. The direct link is <www.gospelcom.net/cgi-ivpress/book.pl/code=3093>.

When leading keep in mind that seekers need to have freedom to come to conclusions themselves. Most of us resist "truth" imposed on us by an authority figure. When group members ask questions, try to direct them back to the text to find the answers themselves. At the same time avoid pressing for responses that are in full agreement with your own answers—or even with the Bible text. Make sure that what the Bible teaches is clear—but allow room for the seeker's opinion.

You may get questions that you don't know how to answer or that are too big for the scope of the session. Sometimes you may need to end the meetings with some questions unanswered. Offer to focus on key areas of questioning in future studies. Don't place yourself under the burden that you have to supply all the answers.

Lead with confidence that the exposure to Scripture and the work of the Spirit will guide group members to the truth. Even if they reject the truth in the end, they will still know it is the truth. And the Spirit will continue to work.

Study 1. Water for the Thirsty. John 4:1-30.

Purpose: To challenge us to overcome the barriers that keep us from talking to other people about Jesus.

General note. If you are leading a group with seekers, see the comments on pages 47-48.

Question 2. You may want to have a large piece of paper ready so that you can work on this as a group. You could also break into small groups of twos and threes and then compare notes.

More people are mentioned in the passage than Jesus, the woman and the disciples of Jesus. Don't forget Jacob (vv. 5, 6, 12), Joseph (Jacob's son; v. 5), the woman's husband (v. 16), and God the Father (vv. 21, 23, 24). You should be prepared to identify these people if members of your group don't know who they are. It is also an opportunity to emphasize the importance of careful observation of the biblical text as we read the Bible.

Question 3. The animosity between Jews and Samaritans had deep historical and religious roots. Seven hundred fifty years before Jesus' day, the Assyrian armies invaded the northern section of Israel and deported the people living there. They left only a few poor Jews in the land. Then the Assyrians imported other conquered people and settled them in the former Jewish territory. The pagan non-Jewish newcomers intermarried with the Jews and produced a mixed racial population called the Samaritans. The Jews both in southern Palestine and in Galilee north of Samaria looked at the Samaritans as a corrupt race and took deliberate steps to remain separate from them. It was the accepted custom that Jews and Samaritans would not drink from the same cup.

By asking for water, Jesus was deliberately crossing several barriers. The first barrier was gender—he talked to a woman. Jewish men were advised never to talk to a woman in public. The second barrier was racial—the woman was a Samaritan; Jesus was a Jew. The third barrier was moral—the woman was living in an immoral relationship with a man she was not married to (v. 18). Jesus was willing to take the risk of crossing those barriers in order to reach a woman who needed to believe in him.

If it's appropriate to your group, you might ask them to think about the internal barriers they have when it comes to talking to others about Jesus. We may fear rejection or we may convince ourselves that we don't know enough about the Bible to answer all their questions. Other barriers might be economics, age or social class. An important element in talking with people about the Lord is timing. Encourage the group to ask God for wisdom to choose the appropriate time to share the gospel message.

Question 4. *Living water* normally referred to running water in a stream or flowing from an underground spring. It was preferred over still water drawn from a well or cistern. Jesus used the image of a spring of water to picture the spiritual refreshment and renewal that would come from a faith relationship with him.

Question 6. The proper place of worship was another issue that separated Jews and Samaritans. Because the Jews in Jerusalem refused to let the Samaritans worship at the temple, the Samaritans built their own temple on Mount Gerizim ("this mountain" in verse 20). The Jews promptly tore down the rival temple of the Samaritans, but worship on Mount Gerizim continued. The hatred between Jews and Samaritans would be resolved only in God's new society, the church (see Acts 8:14-17).

Question 7. The woman had been taught to believe that we try to attract God's attention by our good deeds and pious religious activity. But now Jesus changes her whole perspective by announcing that God is seeking her. Genuine worship does not consist of the repetition of mindless ritual. Genuine worship comes from a spirit of love and adoration for God, and a desire to obey the truth of his Word.

Question 8. Many Christians don't use the opportunities they have to talk about Jesus because they are turned away by external issues. When the disciples saw Jesus talking to the Samaritan woman, they were amazed. Instead of thinking, *He is telling her the good news*, they thought, *Why is Jesus talking to her?* If we are going to see people reached with the gospel, we have to risk being misunderstood or judged even by other Christians. We have to touch some Samaritans!

Question 9. The evidence that the woman genuinely believed in Jesus was not that she took steps to clean up her immoral life (although she certainly did that). The first thing the woman did after coming to faith was tell someone else about Jesus. She didn't have all the answers to their questions. She just pointed them to Christ.

Study 2. Searching for Truth. John 3:1-21.

Purpose: To explore the meaning and importance of the new birth.

General note. If you have seekers in your group, be sure to read the special suggestions about using this guide with them (pp. 47-48).

Question 1. Nicodemus (nick-o-**dee**-mus) knew some facts about Jesus when he first came. He knew that Jesus was a teacher and that he had performed miraculous signs. Nicodemus had also tentatively concluded that Jesus was someone who had come from God as a prophet or messenger. We aren't told if Nicodemus believed in Jesus as God's promised Savior that night, but at some point he did become a follower of Jesus. (See John 19:38-40 where Nicodemus helps bury Jesus after his crucifixion. See also John 7:50-52 where Nicodemus tries to speak in Jesus' defense.)

Question 2. Nicodemus was a member of the Jewish sect called the Pharisees. The Pharisees were devoted to obedience to the law of Moses in the Old Testament. Many of them were so rigid about obedience that they thought God was pleased by rule-keeping more than by an attitude of love for God. Nicodemus was also a member of Israel's ruling religious council, the Sanhedrin. Jesus calls him "Israel's teacher" in verse 10. Nicodemus was a respected Bible scholar.

He may have come to see Jesus at night so that he was less likely to be seen by other Pharisees who looked down on Jesus. It's just as likely that he came at night because that was the best time to have a private talk with Jesus. Nicodemus seems to want to talk about Jesus, but Jesus sees the real reason for his visit—Nicodemus is searching for spiritual fulfilment.

Question 3. Birth is just one picture used in the Bible to portray what results when a person believes in Jesus, but it is a powerful tool for helping people understand the complete transformation Jesus brings. Nicodemus would have put a great deal of trust in his first birth as a member of God's covenant people of Israel. But even the Old Testament Scriptures revealed that more was needed than physical birth into Israel. Men and women needed a new heart—regeneration, transformation, new life from God (Jer 31:33; see also Rom 3:28-29). The only "birth" Nicodemus seemed to be able to imagine was his physical birth as an infant.

Question 4. Jesus wanted Nicodemus to understand that the new birth is spiritual not physical. In order to receive the new birth, a person must be born not only of "water" or "flesh"—that is, born physically—but also of the Spirit. Only God's Spirit can bring life to the human spirit. Birth in the flesh does not get a person into God's kingdom. Entering God's kingdom requires a transforming new act—a second birth—that only God can accomplish.

Question 5. Nicodemus (along with all humanity) had been bitten by the serpent of sin and, as a result, suffered spiritual separation from God (spiritual death). We are not just ignorant and in need of instruction or weak and in need of help. We are spiritually dead and in need of new life. Only by an act of faith could Nicodemus be rescued from the penalty of sin. Jesus was lifted up as the final sacrifice for human sin. When a person looks in faith to Christ, the person receives not what his or her sin deserves but what God in grace gives.

Question 6. Some people picture God as an angry tyrant, waiting to club people who step out of line. Jesus pictured God the Father as a God of mercy who sent his Son to die for human sin and who was determined to save those who believe. So God's primary attitude toward sinful human beings is not condemnation but love. God demonstrated his love by paying the penalty that human sin deserved. Those who refuse to accept God's gracious gift remain under the condemnation of their own sin.

Question 7. Throughout the passage Jesus emphasizes the word *believe*. Belief or faith in its biblical sense is not simply intellectual agreement with certain facts. It is also personal commitment to those facts. The fact is that Jesus died for our sins; faith says that Jesus died for *my* sin, and I rest my confidence for eternal life on what Jesus did. Religious activity and good deeds are not what make us acceptable before God. We are made acceptable by faith alone. Good works flow from a heart of gratitude and love for what God has done for us.

Question 8. God does not force salvation on anyone. He opened the door and provided for us what we could not provide, but we must believe. Those who refuse God's grace demonstrate that they love darkness more than light. Those who refuse to believe in Jesus think they will never be accountable for their evil deeds. Those who receive Christ admit their own sin and find their evil deeds forgiven.

Question 9. Prior to the study, you may want to ask one or two members of the group who are committed Christians to answer this question in the group study session. Don't single out those who are not yet believers. At some point during the weeks of study, you may want to talk privately with any in your group who are unclear about the gospel message or their commitment to Jesus as Saviour and Lord.

Study 3. Caught in the Act. John 8:1-11.

Purpose: To focus on Jesus' compassion toward all of us who are guilty of wrong before God.

General note. In the New International Version of the Bible, this section of John's Gospel (7:53—8:11) is separated from the verses preceding and following by solid lines. The verses are missing from most of the earliest Greek manuscripts of the Gospel of John. Most later manuscripts include the verses (although a few insert them at other places in John, and a few make them part of Luke's Gospel). While the passage raises some textual problems, most evangelical scholars agree with Dr. D. A. Carson who says, "There is little reason for doubting that the event here described occurred, even if in its written form it did not in the beginning belong to the canonical books" (*The Gospel According to John*, Pillar Commentaries; IVP, 1991, p. 333).

Question 3. The Pharisees were one sect or group within first-century Judaism. The Pharisees were vigilant protectors of tradition and the law of Moses. Most of them hated Jesus because Jesus exposed their hypocrisy. Several factors in the passage point to a conspiracy by these religious leaders. (1) When a person commits a sin like adultery, it is usually done in secret, behind locked doors, not in the open. (2) If they caught the woman in the act, there must have been a man involved, but they didn't bring a man *and* a woman, only a woman. (3) These leaders didn't go to the Jewish authorities with the woman. If they really wanted the condemnation of the law carried out, they would have taken her to the Council. (4) Verse 6 says, "They were using this question as a trap, in order to have a basis for accusing him." These men were desperately seeking some way to discredit Jesus before the people.

Question 4. If Jesus simply let the woman go free, the Pharisees could accuse Jesus of breaking and speaking against the law of Moses. Twice the law clearly states that those guilty of adultery are to be stoned (Lev 20:10 and Deut 22:22).

On the other hand, if Jesus agreed that she should be stoned, he would immediately lose his reputation with the people. The people were drawn to Jesus because of his message of grace and forgiveness. If Jesus condemned the woman, he would be just like the Pharisees. Furthermore, if Jesus said she should be stoned, his enemies could use that statement against him in a Roman court. Because Judea was under direct Roman authority, only the Romans could condemn a person to death. If Jesus had pronounced the sentence, he would have defied the Roman government.

Question 5. No one knows what Jesus wrote in the dirt. It's possible that because the Pharisees had come to Jesus as a judge, he was writing his verdict in the dirt before he read it publicly, just a judge in a courtroom would do. He may have been writing accusations against the same men who were accusing the woman. The word John uses in verse 6 means "to write against or to write an accusation." Most likely,

Jesus used the writing as a "stall tactic" to force the men to think more carefully about their accusation and about his challenge to them (v. 7).

Question 6. Jesus' statement (v. 7) forced these men to recognize their own failure to meet every demand of God's law, and to face their own capacity to commit the same sin that the woman had committed.

Question 8. Forgiveness does not grant the person permission to return to or continue in the sinful behavior. Forgiveness gives the person freedom to change without the threat of punishment hanging over him or her. Jesus was not accepting the woman's sin; he was empowering her to change.

Question 9. God's forgiveness is full and free and forever! That forgiveness does not give us license to live a life of sin. Instead it motivates us to live a life of joyful obedience. If Jesus was willing to pay the price for my forgiveness, how can I do less than seek to live fully committed to him?

Question 10. Unfortunately our first response to another Christian who sins is usually like the condemnation of the Pharisees. Jesus, however, wants us to take the time (while he writes in the sand) to reflect on our own failures and to see that we are capable of horrific sin too. Clothed in humility, we are able then to come along beside a friend and help the friend out of the sinful behavior. Our grace does not condone the person's sin but empowers him or her to leave the sin behind.

Study 4. Finding Forgiveness. Luke 7:36-50.

Purpose: To grasp the forgiveness we have in Christ and our responsibility to live lives of gratitude.

Introduction. The account of Chris Carrier's kidnaping and the aftermath comes from a National Public Radio interview broadcast on October 13, 1996. Chris Carrier clearly attributed his ability to forgive his attacker to the Lord's grace in his life.

Question 2. Either Simon thought that Jesus was *not* a prophet and therefore didn't know who the woman was, or he thought that Jesus knew about the woman but didn't care about the rules of the Pharisees that said such a woman's touch made a person unclean. Simon never entertained the possibility that Jesus was a prophet who saw this sinful woman as forgiven and cleansed.

Question 3. Jesus wanted Simon to see that *both* debtors were unable to pay and *both* were forgiven by the grace of the lender. Simon clearly saw the woman's debt to God but couldn't see his own debt. If he had *any* debt to God, he was sure he could take care of it himself by his own religious works.

Question 4. Simon would have greeted each of his Pharisee friends with the customary blessing and washing of their feet. When Jesus came, however, Simon must have refused to extend the same greeting to him. It was a shocking lack of hospitality designed to embarrass Jesus and remind him that he was not part of Simon's circle of trusted friends.

Question 5. The woman had probably had some contact with Jesus before she came to the banquet room. Perhaps she had heard him teaching or had even talked privately with him. She knew that Jesus would not reject her, but she risked Simon's rebuke by showing up unannounced and uninvited.

Question 6. The answers to this question will reveal a lot about how the members of your group see themselves before God. Be sensitive to those who see themselves as unforgiven or unforgivable. The purpose of this whole study is to point that person to the one who is anxious to forgive.

Question 8. Ask the group to imagine themselves in her position and to express the sense of freedom and joy that must have flooded her spirit. You may also want to point out that her *actions* toward Jesus were not the basis of her salvation. Jesus said, "Your faith has saved you" (v. 50). Her actions were expressions of gratitude for Jesus' love and cleansing.

Question 9. Jesus does not lecture this woman on how she is to clean up her life. Jesus realizes that one mark of true forgiveness is the desire to demonstrate our gratitude by living in obedience to God. The woman was motivated to change her life because of her love for Jesus, not because a list of rules was imposed on her.

Question 10. The woman did not really care about what the people in the banquet room thought about her. She was only concerned that Jesus would know how much she loved him. She responded to Jesus' grace with a spontaneous, extravagant act of love and sacrifice. Unfortunately, most of us are more like Simon. We are cold and calculating in our expression of love to Jesus. We are more concerned about what others think of us than that Jesus would know how much we love him.

Study 5. Facing Failure. John 21:1-19.
Purpose: To explore Jesus' attitude toward us when we fail and his willingness to restore us to a place of usefulness in his work.
Question 1. Move through these questions rapidly to overview the passage, but challenge the group to think beyond the most obvious answers to these questions. The disciples were certainly frustrated and disappointed because they didn't catch any fish, but they were also hungry and tired. A few months earlier, when Jesus had predicted his own death, Peter had rebuked the Lord (Mt 16:21-23). Now as he heard Jesus talk about the death he would have to die, Peter listened with humility and seriousness.
Question 2. See Mark 1:16-20 for the account of how Jesus called these disciples. At that time they left their fishing behind to follow him.
Question 3. The disciples weren't far from shore, but in the pre-dawn darkness they couldn't see who was talking to them. When they felt the nets fill at the man's command, the disciple John ("the disciple whom Jesus loved," v. 7) realized that the speaker had to be Jesus.
Question 4. Jesus' servant attitude continued even after his resurrection from the dead. Before his death, Jesus had washed the disciples' feet as an act of humble service (Jn 13:1-17).
Question 5. Recall Peter's denial of Jesus (described in the introduction) after his boastful claim a few days earlier that he would never abandon Jesus. Jesus, of course, knew Peter's heart and mind, but he asked these questions to get the relationship out in the open, to clear the air of any tension that might still be lingering between them. Jesus gave Peter the opportunity to declare his love for Jesus openly so that he could be restored to leadership among Jesus' followers.

John's Gospel was originally composed in Greek, the universal language of the New Testament world. In his question to Peter, Jesus used the Greek verb *agapao*. In his answer to Jesus, Peter used the verb *phileo*. The third time Jesus asked the question, he also used the verb *phileo*.

Some scholars believe that John used the two words as synonyms and that it was just a stylistic feature to interchange the words. Other students of John think the word change was intentional. The word *agapao* means "to choose to love and to commit oneself sacrificially to the person loved." *Phileo* is generally used to describe a love based on relationship and emotional attachment, a love that strengthens or weakens depending on circumstances. Even though Peter's love had not become all that Jesus wanted it to be, Jesus is still willing to use Peter in ministry and service.

Question 7. Jesus' use of Peter's word for love gives the question a different emphasis. "Are you sure, Peter, that you have even that level of love for me?" Peter was saddened by Jesus' question, but he had to honestly admit that the most he would claim for himself at this point was that he had genuine affection for Jesus.

Question 8. Emphasize with the group that Jesus responds positively to whatever level of allegiance we have to him. Jesus always comes with grace to a person who is open to him. Jesus' grace and love draw us closer to him and give us a desire to love him more.

Question 9. When we admit our failure to the Lord and seek to live obediently, the Lord restores us to a place of ministry and involvement in his kingdom. Other Christians may not be as willing to see a Christian who has failed restored to usefulness, but the Lord will open doors of opportunity to tend God's flock if we are sensitive to his guidance.

Study 6. Set Free. Mark 5:1-20.
Purpose: To help us recognize the reality of Satan and his demons, and the power of Jesus to set us free from their oppression.
Group discussion. Jesus (and the New Testament writers) portrayed Satan and demons as real beings. These evil angelic beings attack Christians and non-Christians, and seek to "demonise" them in any way possible. Some in your group may think that Jesus was just accommodating himself to a popular explanation for serious psychiatric problems. Jesus, however, never accepted popular beliefs about anything if those beliefs weren't true. Jesus had no problem exposing falsehood or popularly held myths. Why would he hesitate to expose

a belief in demons as untrue? Instead, Jesus clearly taught about and acted toward demons as real spirit beings.

Question 1. If not everyone works, suggest some other context: in your classes, at your child's school and so on.

Question 3. Most of us would pray that someone would set this man free from the oppression he lived under. The focus throughout this study should not be so much on demons but on the liberating power of Jesus and the transformation of every life Jesus touches.

Question 4. The man was controlled by many demons (v. 9). They were able to direct his speech and his actions, and even impart supernatural strength to his body. People can be "demonised" to different degrees and on different levels, but Satan's control (exercised through demons) is always pictured as oppression and bondage.

Question 5. The Bible never pictures the spiritual conflict as a battle between equals. God has dominion over his entire universe, including Satan. Even though the demons were stronger than a human being, they recognized that they were no match for Jesus.

If the group struggles with the second part of the question, try rewording this way: "The demons could do nothing without Jesus' permission. What does that tell you about the power of evil angels compared with Jesus' power?"

Question 6. This question may prompt a whole range of answers. It is important to anchor the answers in the statements of Scripture. This might also be a good place to warn those in the group of excessive interest in demons. Satan and his angels are defeated enemies! But they are not to be taken lightly either. Strong faith, spiritual maturity and trust in the power of Jesus alone are necessary when we face demons.

Question 7. Jesus agreed to the requests of the demons and the people but said no to the man he had set free! Jesus wanted the man to go back to his own home area with the good news of his deliverance by the power of God.

Question 8. Jesus' power brought a complete transformation of the man's life. The change was obvious to anyone looking on. Furthermore, the man was willing to do what Jesus asked him to do. Joyful obedience marked his life.

Question 9. As the leader, you will most likely need to get this discussion started. My opinion is that a genuine believer in Jesus who is indwelt by the Holy Spirit cannot at the same time be possessed by an evil spirit. Christians can, however, be demonized to varying degrees depending on their willingness to give Satan a foothold through disobedience or complacency. If a Christian has tolerated sin or disobedience to God in his or her life, the door may be open to demonic influence.

Study 7. Seeing the Light. John 9:1-38.

Purpose: To encourage us to follow Christ even at the risk of rejection or opposition.

Question 2. The disciples had been taught that physical deformity or defect was the direct result of the parents' sin or the baby's sin. Even an unborn child could commit acts of willful sin—and the evidence was the baby's kicking in the mother's womb! The disciples' question was understandable, but their attitude was not. They did not look at the man with compassion or care. He was just another theological case-study. Jesus looked at him as a person with feelings and hurts. More than that, Jesus saw him as a man afflicted with spiritual blindness—a blindness far worse in its consequences than his physical blindness.

Jesus' answer to the disciples reveals that God takes full responsibility for the way he has made us. There are no mistakes in God's sovereign plan (see Ex 4:11 and Eph 1:11). Jesus' remark that "neither this man nor his parents sinned" does not mean, of course, that they were sinless. He meant that the man's blindness was not the direct result of anyone's specific sin.

Question 3. Even if a person has a perfect body and a brilliant mind, that person is separated from God by personal sin. Only God's grace and power can rescue us from sin's dominion and restore us to friendship with God.

Question 4. This is one of the few times that Jesus does not instantly heal a person simply with a touch or command. Perhaps Jesus wanted to begin to awaken faith in the man so he would later believe in Jesus as Savior. The man was willing to obey what Jesus said even though he had no idea who Jesus was. Maybe it was because Jesus took the time to minister to him and show concern for him while everyone else saw him as a nuisance.

Question 5. The Pharisees were a sect within Judaism. They were committed to the strict observance of the Old Testament law. When Jesus made clay and smeared it on the man's eyes, he was working on the sabbath day! The Pharisees never considered the power or significance of the miracle. The fact that Jesus broke their rules convinced them that Jesus could not be from God. Jesus repeatedly healed on the sabbath to demonstrate that works of compassion are always within God's will. These Pharisees had already written Jesus off as an imposter. They refused to honestly evaluate Jesus' claims to be the promised Deliverer (v. 22).

Question 6. The man who had been blind now sees! The men who claimed to be a light for God are revealed to be spiritually blind. It is possible to claim to "see" but still be in spiritual darkness.

Question 7. The only thing these Pharisees got excited about was someone breaking the rules! Christians can get so calloused to the wonder of God's grace that we quietly yawn our way through worship or casually dismiss a great work of God's power.

Question 8. The most effective response the man had to the critics and skeptics was his joyful personal account of what Jesus had done in his life. The man was not a religious scholar, but he had come to the correct conclusions about Jesus based on what had happened in his life. He didn't know yet who Jesus was, but he *did* know that Jesus had changed his life. The only answer the Pharisees had to his testimony was to throw him out (v. 34)!

Question 9. Jesus came to the man again because, even though he wasn't blind physically anymore, he was still blind spiritually. The man had come to certain conclusions about Jesus, but he had not yet believed in Jesus as Savior and Lord. He gave evidence of his faith by a verbal expression of his trust in Jesus and by genuine worship of Jesus as Lord and God (v. 38).

Study 8. When All Else Fails. Luke 8:40-48.

Purpose: To demonstrate Jesus' concern for one individual in need and his power to change impossible situations.

Group discussion. You may want to begin by reading the introduction out loud and then asking the group to respond to the discussion question. The purpose of the question is not to come up with the "right" answer but to get the members of your group to wrestle with a difficult situation.

Question 1. Try to bring out the emotional undertones in each speaker. Encourage the members of the group to put themselves in each person's place and to think about how they would feel.

Question 2. The author of the Gospel was a physician named Luke (Col 4:14). His commentary is that the woman "had been subject to bleeding for twelve years" (Lk 8:43). Apparently the woman was afflicted with a constant menstrual flow. Luke further adds that "no one could heal her." Mark's account says, "She had suffered a great deal under the care of many doctors and had spent all she had, yet instead of getting better she grew worse" (Mk 5:26).

Question 3. Because blood and the life it represented were central ideas in the sacrifices offered to the Lord, the Old Testament law declared that contact with blood made a person ceremonially unclean. Certain restrictions were placed an anyone who touched blood or had a bodily discharge of blood. The complex regulations of Leviticus 10—15 were designed to demonstrate the "separateness" of God from impurity and the "separateness" of the nation of Israel from the pagan people around them.

The woman in Luke 8 risked the displeasure of the people around her, since touching a person who was ritually unclean would make them unclean for a period of time. The woman may have avoided approaching Jesus directly out of fear that he would be unwilling to touch and heal someone who was ceremonially unclean. Jesus, however, never hesitated to approach and touch people considered untouchable. He healed many who had skin diseases like leprosy, and he often healed them with a touch. (See, for example, Lk 5:12-14.)

Question 4. The woman was fearful that Jesus might turn her away if she came to him directly. But she was also confident that Jesus had the power to heal her. She believed that just touching the edge of his outer cloak would bring relief and cleansing.

Question 7. It seems cruel at first that Jesus forced this woman to reveal herself and her condition. Jesus, however, had more to accomplish in her life than physical healing. He certainly wanted to affirm her faith in him as the source of power to overcome life's problems. He also wanted to use her testimony as a witness to the crowd of who he was. Jesus also used the opportunity to declare her cleansing publicly. Under the Old Testament law, when a person who was ceremonially unclean was cleansed, a priest publicly announced the person's reception back into Israel's worship (Lev 14:11).

Question 8. The woman was certainly released from the emotional drain of a lingering illness. She also was set free from the social stigma and embarrassment of her affliction. The members of your group will probably have several more good answers.

Now or Later. Use these questions as a wrap-up of the whole series of studies. Focus on the group's expanded perception of Jesus and how they have been changed by these encounters with him.

Douglas Connelly is a Christian writer and speaker who lives with his wife, Karen, near Flint, Michigan. He is the author of Angels Around Us *and* The Promise of Heaven *(InterVarsity Press) and* The Bible for Blockheads *(Zondervan) as well as a number of LifeBuilder Bible Studies.*

Other LifeBuilder Bible Studies by Douglas Connelly
Angels
Daniel
Heaven
John
Mary (with Karen Connelly)
Meeting the Spirit
Miracles

Additional resources to use in leading these studies are available on the Web page for this book at <www.ivpress.com>. The direct link is <www.gospelcom.net/cgi-ivpress/book.pl/code=3093>. Resources include video clip ideas and a chart comparing the Gospels.

What Should We Study Next?

A good place to continue your study of Scripture would be with a book study. Many groups begin with a Gospel such as *Mark* (20 studies by Jim Hoover) or *John* (26 studies by Douglas Connelly). These guides are divided into two parts so that if twenty or twenty-six weeks seems like too much to do at once, the group can feel free to do half and take a break with another topic. Later you might want to come back to it. You might prefer to try a shorter letter. *Philippians* (9 studies by Donald Baker), *Ephesians* (11 studies by Andrew T. and Phyllis J. Le Peau) and *1 & 2 Timothy and Titus* (11 studies by Pete Sommer) are good options. If you want to vary your reading with an Old Testament book, consider *Ecclesiastes* (12 studies by Bill and Teresa Syrios) for a challenging and exciting study.

There are a number of interesting topical LifeBuilder studies as well. Here are some options for filling three or four quarters of a year:

Basic Discipleship
Christian Beliefs, 12 studies by Stephen D. Eyre
Christian Character, 12 studies by Andrea Sterk & Peter Scazzero
Christian Disciplines, 12 studies by Andrea Sterk & Peter Scazzero
Evangelism, 12 studies by Rebecca Pippert & Ruth Siemens

Building Community
Christian Community, 10 studies by Rob Suggs
Fruit of the Spirit, 9 studies by Hazel Offner
Spiritual Gifts, 12 studies by Charles & Anne Hummel

Character Studies
David, 12 studies by Jack Kuhatschek
New Testament Characters, 12 studies by Carolyn Nystrom
Old Testament Characters, 12 studies by Peter Scazzero
Women of the Old Testament, 12 studies by Gladys Hunt

The Trinity
Meeting God, 12 studies by J. I. Packer
Meeting Jesus, 13 studies by Leighton Ford
Meeting the Spirit, 12 studies by Douglas Connelly